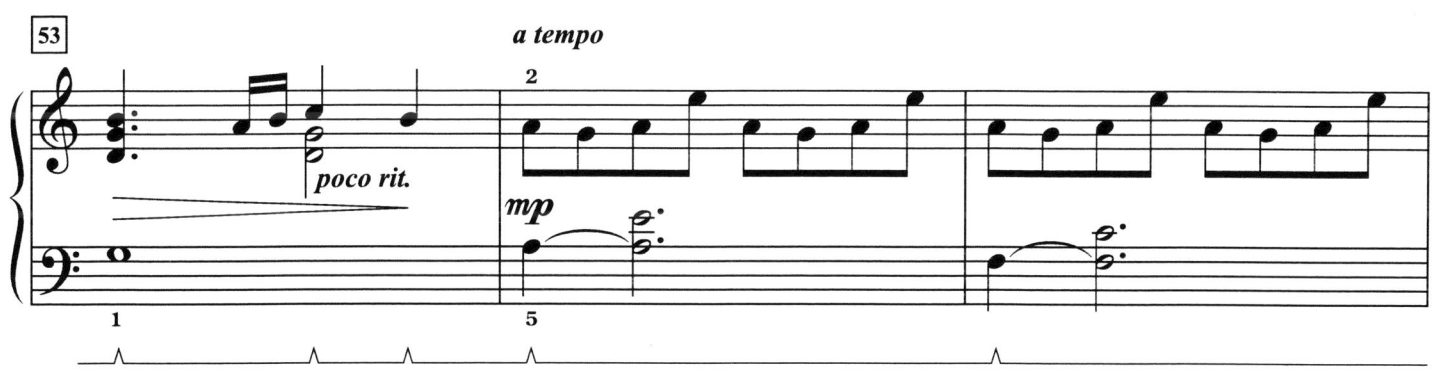

10,000 Reasons
(Bless the Lord)

Bless the Lord, O my soul: and all that is within me, bless his holy name.
— Psalm 103:1 (KJV)

(Approx. Performance Time – 2:30)

Words and Music by
Matt Redman and Jonas Myrin
Arr. Carol Tornquist

© 2011 SHOUT! PUBLISHING (APRA) (Administered in the U.S. and Canada at CapitolCMGPublishing.com), THANKYOU MUSIC (PRS)
(Administered worldwide at CapitolCMGPublishing.com excluding Europe which is Administered. by kingswaysongs.com), WORSHIPTOGETHER.
COM SONGS, SIXSTEPS MUSIC and SAID AND DONE MUSIC (Administered at CapitolCMGPublishing.com)
All Rights Reserved   Used by Permission

(Approx. Performance Time – 2:15)

Forever Reign

The Lord reigns, he is robed in majesty;
indeed, the world is established, firm and secure.
Your throne was established long ago; you are from all eternity.

—Psalm 93:1–2 (NIV)

Words and Music by
Jason Ingram and Reuben Morgan
Arr. Carol Tornquist

© 2009 HILLSONG MUSIC PUBLISHING, WEST MAIN MUSIC, WINDSOR HILL MUSIC and SONY/ATV TIMBER PUBLISHING
All Rights for HILLSONG MUSIC PUBLISHING Administered at CapitolCMGPublishing.com
All Rights Reserved   Used by Permission